UNDERCOVER
GENERATION

Other books by Raphael Grant:

Another Level of Prayer

Still Standing

Principles of Purpose and Adversity

Breaking Satanic Cycles

Strategic Prayer

Enemy at the Gate

UNDERCOVER GENERATION

The Unassuming Generation That Is Rising Up To Take Over

RAPHAEL GRANT

Rev. date: 05/26/2021

To order additional copies of this book, contact:
Xlibris
844-714-8691
www.Xlibris.com
Orders@Xlibris.com
830120

Contents

I am dedicating this book to my boys Zuriel and Zephan,

I love you guys so much,you are my inspiration,

and also to you my queen, my best friend Aretha,

forever in love with you.

Introduction

One day the Lord showed me a revelation of thousands of worshippers who were worshipping in a dome like a stadium, and I saw so many people dancing and singing, very ecstatic, but the astonishing thing about that revelation was that while I was looking on the worshippers in the dome, I saw Christ standing outside the dome, where the worship was going on, and then the revelation ended.

This revelation troubled me because I didn't understand why Christ was standing outside and not inside where the worshippers were because the scripture says, "*He inhabits the praise of His people,*" so I expected Him to be part of the thousands of worshippers or to be in the midst of them.

"*But thou art Holy, O thou that inhabits the praises of Israel*" (Ps. 22:3).

The Holy Spirit began to speak to me, and he said some of the revival, conferences, services that we have in our churches that we think Christ is part of it. He is not and it's just a religious gathering. That amazed me. The spirit of the Lord continued to speak to me that instead of the church sweeping the world, the world is rather sweeping the church, and the church has gone worldly while the world had now gone churchly. So you can't even distinguish between the church and the world any longer. That is the reason why we are not experiencing the move of God, and our churches have been dry and void of power and miracles. People come into church sick and leave sicker.

Our messages are no longer about the Holy Spirit; it's no longer about Christ, and the word of God is all about man-made theology and self-help messages based on motivation, believing in self, human philosophy, ideology, and methodology.

There is a rising generation that is not worldly. They have gone through the process, and they have been refined and polished by the process and getting ready to take over; they are world changers, community transformers, and continent shakers.

I remember many years ago as a teenager, I was waiting on the Lord, and while praying, the Lord opened my eyes and I saw a multitude of people who were dark in appearance walking on the same path, going the same direction, and I heard a voice from the clouds that were above them asking me, "Do you know these people, and do you know where they are going?" I responded and said I have no idea where they are going, and the voice of the Lord from the clouds told me, "They are all going to hell." That frightened me because I couldn't believe so many people are going to hell. The spirit of the Lord told me to pick a dairy and start writing what He is going to tell me, and so I did as I was commanded. And some of the things that He told me were that most of the ministers He called have failed Him because they have relegated their primary call to the background, which is the winning of souls. He called them to fish men, but now they are fishing for fame, accolades, and prosperity.

The ministers are competing among themselves, who has the largest congregation and who is driving the latest model of cars, and it has become all about themselves and not God or the assignment He has given them.

When the Lord told me all these things, it suddenly dawned on me why the church is powerless and the presence of the Holy Spirit is no longer in our services, and Christ is not part of our meetings and so-called revival conferences. These are the reasons why God is raising an undercover generation, to fulfill His purpose before His return as the king of kings and the lord of lords.

This is the generation I call the unassuming and the unpredictable. This is a generation that carries His presence and power, a generation that is undefiled, a generation that seeks after God.

"This is the generation of them that seek Him, that seek thy face o Jacob" (Ps. 24:6).

I crave your indulgence as we take the journey together through the pages of this book, to discover who the undercover generation is and why the undercover generation.

Chapter 1

Undercover Generation

Anything that is undercover means the real identity of that thing is concealed, is surreptitious, and covert. It also means operating in a way so as to ensure complete concealment and confidentiality, cloak-and-dagger activities behind enemy lines.

When somebody is undercover, the person can look ordinary yet be extraordinary; it goes beyond what is seen on the surface.

This undercover generation is a hidden generation and the reason is that because most of the fathers have failed as fathers in their responsibilities and mentorship to the sons and daughters, and when I talk about fathers here, I am talking about spiritual fathers, those that God has positioned in the kingdom to help the younger generation with their experience and their process to where they are.

Today, sonship to a father in the kingdom is dependent on the fatness of your tithe and offering. If you can't bring fat offering and tithe, you are not accepted as a son, and so it's all about what they can get. And even when you bring the fat offering, they will still not mentor, guide, and teach you anything because they think mentoring you will make you better and greater than them, which is how it's supposed to be. Unfortunately it's not.

There are so many sons and daughters that are looking for fathers, and they can't find any because of the exploitation and abuse, and so what God is doing now is He is raising men and women and He is training them and processing and mentoring them Himself through the power of the Holy Spirit. These men and women are undercover; they are not known, they are not on television, and they are not popular and famous. Most of them don't even have any background, and the reason why God is training these men and women undercover is because He doesn't want the enemy to detect them and also doesn't want them to be corrupted by the world and the things of the world.

"And there arose another generation after them" (Judg. 2:10a).

A generation is rising who will understand scripture and the supernatural, they are the children of the end-time. The elect overcomers of the last days and perhaps the chosen inheritors of heavens greatest harvest. A grand and glorious army, rising up to take over, conquer, and also overcome satanic powers, demonic entities, and territorial powers. The undercover generation is ordinary lives being moved by an extraordinary God.

This is a growing segment of believers with a different perspective of Christian living. They accept the word of God for what it is and live life assertively, seizing the kingdom of God by force without a second thought. Their passion is to take kingdoms, impact communities, spiritual warfare, soul-winning, intercession, fasting, and prayers. These are a new breed of believers who know their purpose and achieve results.

The undercover generation will not cease to stop until they experience the power of God. This particular generation, I mean *the undercover generation,* they live for His glory and are sustained by His presence. They are completely distinguished from any other people. *The undercover generation* is not contaminated by yesterday's ideology, methodologies, and man's traditions. They are radicals and flexible to change. They are willing to do whatever it takes to get *kingdom business* done.

This undercover generation can be likened to that of a steam roller, crushing anything in its path that doesn't yield vitality and productivity. The bottom line is the manifestation, results! The kind of zeal they possess, if unharmed, will turn the world upside down. Principled training is key to the proper channeling of their energies and attaining results. There's no better training resource for these avid individuals than the Holy Spirit. This is the generation that is not interested in the *status quo* but rather those people who want an adventurous and fruitful

Christian walk. These are people of power and presence, they live and walk in the supernatural, and it has become the norm.

In this end-time, the undercover generation will demolish its enemy. They will rise without an established precedent and with the ability to break and take dominion over all evil deeds. The undercover generation will also rise as the answer to the wave of *filth* and *sin* that are dominating the human race and the church. These are people who have been injected by God with a fresh sense of urgency; they can no longer afford to sleep anymore for the time is short. These are believers who have cast aside every weight and sin to attain the necessary spiritual heights.

This is the generation that has realized through divine training by the Holy Spirit that Christianity is not a game, but a titanic conflict against the forces of darkness. These individuals are very militant in their attitudes, and the world is beginning to feel the impact of a new species of God's people. God has raised this undercover generation to carry out the enormous divine program to save a sinking world. You are a part of the undercover generation. If you are not, I trust that as you read this book you will be supernaturally transformed into a patriot of God.

God is raising up a new generation of men and women with the tenacity of a bulldog and the bodacious personality of a lion in the areas of government, politics, education, culture, economics, theater, business, and sports. They are absolutely and completely committed to fulfilling His will and purpose in their lives. God is working with these people using them in different ways. Let us look at spiritual examples of this.

"For David, after he had served his own generation by the will of God, fell asleep, was buried with his fathers, and saw corruption" (Acts 13:36).

> *For He is our God, and we are the people of his pasture, and the sheep of his hand.*
>
> *Today if ye will hear his voice, harden not your heart, as in the provocation, and as in the day of temptation in the wilderness.*
>
> *When your Fathers tempted me, proved me, and saw my work.*
>
> *Forty years long I grieved with this generation and said, it is a people that do err in their heart, and they have not known my ways.*
>
> *Unto whom I sware in my wrath that they should not enter into my rest.* (Ps. 95: 7–11)

In these verses of the scripture, we see the example of a generation that deviated from God's original plan. We know this to be true because many of their celebrations became traditions and religious performances, plans designed by men, not by God.

"I will give children to be their princes, and babes shall rule over them" (Isa. 3:4).

The undercover generation is composed of young apostles, prophets, evangelists, pastors, and teachers. Today, many of the elders in the church stand in the way of God's plans. They are no longer a blessing to the body of Christ. Due to this, God has chosen the younger generation called the undercover generation.

I'm not ignoring the fact that God has preserved a remnant of a few men and women who are older and wiser; they hold generations together. They build the bridge, closing the gap between the new and old generations. I have divinely come in contact with many elderly, wise men and women that recognize that they are instruments that God is using to ease the transition between the old and the new generations. They are not envious of the undercover generation. They are willing and desperate to find people to teach them everything they know. This is how new disciples will be trained and how they will receive the impartation of the old wine as they walk into the dimension of the new wine.

> And no man putteth new into old bottles, else the new wine will burst the bottles and be spilled, and the bottles shall perish.
> But new wine must be put into new bottles; and both are preserved.

No man also having drunk old wine straightway desireth

new; for he saith, the old is better. (Luke 5:37–39)

God is raising a new generation, the undercover generation, to carry on a radical revolution which will change the spiritual climate and release His glory. This is a radical revolution that will overturn and overthrow human traditions from the church. This new rising generation is bringing the body of Christ back to an emphasis on the power of the Holy Spirit and the word of God. This move of the Holy Spirit is introducing a new breed of believers into the kingdom of God. Much of the features of this move of the spirit are, however, often misunderstood and misinterpreted by the onlooking world. This rising generation operates in an unusual power; they know how to yield to the Holy Spirit. They are carriers of His presence, the container of His glory, their faces are like that of a lion, spiritually speaking. Air can be polluted with chemicals, dust, and many other physical things. But one group of air pollutants that are very dangerous not only to the body but also to the spirit and soul are negative words. Words that cause fear, suspicion, unbelief, and sin are pollutants. Jesus speaking to his audience said, *"Take heed what ye year"* (Mark 4:24).

It is important to realize how not to allow anything, just anything, to get into your spirit. Be selective about what you hear.

"Take heed therefore how ye hear" (Luke 18:18).

1.1 Why Undercover Generation

Today the body of Christ has been traditionalized and full of human agenda and philosophy. There is no revival. As a result, there is no power, and prayerlessness in the church has resulted in the church-going, worldly people and full of carnality. The church is more excited about fleshly things than spiritual things. The church is a spiritual institution, and it is managed and operated by the Holy Spirit. Our prayerlessness and worldliness are proof and evidence that we are now strangers to the power and manifestation of the Holy Spirit.

How can the church in its ignorance abandon the Holy Spirit which is the divine instructor of the Church. The Church today is struggling for survival. The fact is that the church has been caught naked. She has not the power she talks of, or she is probably sick and cannot display that power. The church today trails in poverty when riches in Christ are hers. She seems to be in flight instead of in a fight. We have a stricken church in a stricken world. The most embarrassing thing is that we have no one to blame for our spiritual impotence.

We have not half a chance that anyone will believe us for transferring to another the guilt of our criminal stagnation. We cannot blame the devil for this impasse because Jesus said, *"I give unto you power . . . over all the power of the enemy."* We cannot blame our enemies because the word says, *"We are more than conquerors through him that loved us."* We cannot blame the weapons combined against us because we have the shield of faith. *"Wherewith ye shall be able to quench all the fiery darts of the wicked."* We dare not blame God for the stagnation of the church, because He has said, *"Ask, and it shall be given you."* We cannot say the supply lines have run out because the scriptures say, *"All things are yours."* The church has no excuse for its state right now.

1.2 A Hungry Generation

This is a generation that wants more of God, desires His presence. They are not satisfied with what they are seeing in the church, the dryness, the powerlessness, the entertainment, scripture-less preaching and teachings. I have realized by experiential knowledge that change comes when people are discontent and dissatisfied in certain aspects of their life, such as the spiritual level and dimension they find themselves in. Discontent causes a hunger deep in your heart, which reveals the things you need to learn and know. Pain compels change and revivals. Painful experiences cause traditions and obsolete mentalities to change. God is bringing change to His church, He is bringing up a new generation with a new anointing.

In the Old Testament and the New, you see the older generation impacting into the new generation, which is why when you see an Abraham, you will see an Isaac, and anytime you see Isaac, you will see a Jacob. Anytime you see a Jacob, you will see a Joseph. The next generation, anytime you see a Moses, you will see a Joshua. When you see a Joshua, you will see an Elijah. When you see Elijah, you will see an Elisha. When you see a David, you will see a Solomon. When you see a Naomi, you will see a Ruth. When you see an Eli, you will see a Samuel. When you see a Jesus, you will see the twelve disciples, and finally when you see a Paul, you will see a Timothy.

And so both in the Old and New Testaments, there has been that transfer of anointing and mentoring, but in this generation, there is none. Hardly will you find a true mentor that is willing to transfer, impact, and also teach the ways of God. That is why this generation is hungry for more of God. What the undercover generation knows is by divine inspiration and teachings of the Holy Spirit.

1.3 Undercover Personalities

These undercover personalities had no background, some of them nobody knows where they are coming from, they just showed up.

ELIJAH

"And Elijah the Tishbite, who was of the inhabitants of Gilead, said unto Ahab, As the Lord God of Israel liveth, before whom I stand, there shall not be dew nor rain these years according to my word" (1 Kings 17:1).

"And Elijah the Tishbite, who was of the inhabitants of Gilead" (verse 1). Notice how Elijah just suddenly appeared on the scene. We are told little about him. He simply emerges out of obscurity from the standpoint of the record of scripture. Nothing is mentioned about his parents, his ancestry, training, or early life. He is simply called "the Tishbite who was of the inhabitants of Gilead." In other words, he was not on Israel's who-is-who list. He was known as a prophet as the account that follows suggests. However, scripture places very little emphasis on his background, yet when he showed up, he was declaring and decreeing the word of the Lord with boldness and without fear or intimidation. Locking up the heavens and declaring there will be no rain according to his word, and it was so as he spoke it.

Elijah was an uncover prophet who took the devil by surprise and the nation of Israel by storm because he was undercover. The devil couldn't locate him, and not only that, the devil couldn't figure him out. He challenged the status quo of his day a time when the majority of the Israelites has gone into the worship of an idol called Baal. Elijah challenged the prophets of Baal to a contest, saying, *"Let the God that answers by Fire, let him be God."*

Elijah prophesied and it was so. He decreed things and it was established, turn the heart of the Israelite back to God. Elijah was one of the greatest prophets that ever lived, so anointed and powerful that he couldn't see death.

"And was transfigured before them; and his face did shine as the sun, and his raiment was white as the light. And, behold there appeared unto them Moses and Elias talking with him" (Matt. 17:2–3).

Elijah appearing at the mount of transfiguration represents the prophets and the spirit, and Moses appearing represents the law, the Word. There were so many people in scripture that God kept undercover even in the time of Elijah when he taught he was the only one who had not bowed to Baal.

"Yet I have left me seven thousand in Israel, all the knees which have now bowed to Baal, and every month which had kissed him" (1 Kings 19:18).

And so there were seven thousand people that God kept undercover, who had not defiled themselves by bowing to Baal or kissing Baal, and Elijah knew it not.

The purpose for the undercover generation is for God to keep a generation for Himself that has not entangled with the corruption of this world, a generation that understands they are in this world but are not of this world. *"Lord, they have killed thy prophets, and digged down thine altars, and I am left alone, and they seek my life.*

"But what saith the answer of God unto him? I have reserved to myself seven thousand men, who have not bowed the knee to the image of baal." (Rom. 11: 3–4).

STEPHEN

He was an undercover prophet who nobody knew where he comes from. His parents, nobody knew where he came from; nobody knew. The first time his name was mentioned, he was arranging tables.

"Wherefore, brethren, look ye out among you seven men of honest report, full of the Holy Ghost and wisdom, whom we may appoint over this business, but we will give ourselves continually to prayer, and to the ministry of the word. And the saying pleased the whole multitude and they chose Stephen, a man full of faith and of the Holy Ghost and Philip, and Prochorus, and Nimon, and Timon, and Parmenas, and Nicholas a proselyte of Antioch" (Acts 6:3–5).

He wasn't one of the apostles who had been with Jesus from the beginning. He wasn't popular or famous, but he was full of the Holy Spirit and of power; the Spirit of God taught him, mentored him, and also taught him the ways of God. When nobody had an idea who Stephen was and who he will become because he was undercover and he wasn't prematurely exposed, the devil couldn't figure him out. By the time he realized it, Stephen was already on the scene doing exploits for God, stopping the mouths of lions, shutting the mouth of the serpent, fighting wild beast, running through a troop, leaping over walls with the Gospel of Jesus Christ, teaching and preaching the uncompromising and unadulterated word of God of which the sycophants of his day and time couldn't handle. When you are undercover, you don't compromise in your convictions, you are steadfast and resilient, unmovable.

Stephen wasn't even one of the apostles. He was just a deacon with no background, yet God used him mightily. In fact the church didn't choose him to preach or teach, the church chose him among seven others to take care of the widows and the needy people in Jerusalem, who were neglected. God used him to perform miracles and at the time of his death, Jesus stood and gave him a standing ovation, meaning "I am proud of you, dying for the gospel." In fact, Stephen was the first martyr of the gospel.

"As they heard this they were enraged in their hearts and gnashed their teeth at him, but he, full of the Holy Spirit, looked up into heaven and saw the glory of God and Jesus standing at God's right hand and said, 'I see the heavens opened and the son of man standing at God's right hand'" (Acts 7:54 –56).

MELCHIZEDEK

It simply means *"King of righteousness or King of Salem (peace) and a priest of the most high God,"* Melchizedek is introduced in scripture as a man without a father, without a mother, without a descendant, has no beginning, and has no end. This is a peculiarity of Messiah's priesthood that is not derived from another before Him and passes it on to another after Him.

"Also there were many priests who because they were prevented by death from continuing. But He, because He continues forever has unchangeable priesthood" (Heb. 7:23–24)

Without father refers to Melchizedek officially not naturally. He was independent of his descent unlike the Aaronic priests, who forfeited the priesthood if they could not trace their descent.

"These sought their listing among those who were registered b genealogy, but it was not found, therefore there were excluded from the priesthood as defile.

"And the governor said to them that they should not eat of the most holy things till a priest could consult with the Urim and Thummim" (Neh. 7:64–65).

Melchizedek had no fixed beginning or end of his king priesthood, such as the Levitical priests who began at thirty and ended at fifty years of age.

"For every high priest is appointed to offer both gifts and sacrifices. Therefore it is necessary that this one also have something to offer" (Heb. 8:3).

According to the scripture above, it proves for blessing and tithing, which alone are recorded, are not enough to constitute priesthood. Abraham The friend of God recognized him (probably having received some divine intimation) at once as his spiritual superior and this in a day when every patriarch was the priest of his family. *"And Melchizedek,*

King of Salem brought forth bread and wine and he was the priest of the most high God.

"And he blessed him and said, blessed be Abram of the most high God, possessor of heaven and earth.

"And blessed be the most high God, which hath delivered thine enemies into thy hand. And he gave him tithes of all" (Gen. 14:18–20).

Melchizedek disappears as suddenly as he came, undercover, a type of Christ. Almost a thousand years elapsed before the next notice of Melchizedek.

"The Lord hath sworn, and will not repent, thou (Messiah) art a priest forever after the order of Melchizedek" (Ps. 110:4).

The Aaronic priesthood was made after the law of a carnal commandment, but the Melchizedek priesthood is after the power of an endless life as is declared a thousand years later than the psalm.

> *For this Melchisedec, king of Salem, priest of the most high God, who met Abraham returning from the slaughter of the kings, and blessed him.*
>
> *To whom also Abraham gave a tenth part of all; first being by interpretation King of righteousness, and after that also King of Salem, which is, King of peace;*

Without father, without mother, without descent, having

neither beginning of days, nor end of life; but made like

unto the Son of God; abideth a priest continually

And it is yet far more evident, for that after similitude of

Melchisedec there ariseth another priest. (Heb. 7:1–3, 15)

Melchisedec, unlike Aaronic priesthood, did not receive his priesthood by inheritance, because the Messiah was not a Levi, but a Judah. He did not transmit it to any successor. The priesthood of Aaron ended as recorded in the New Testament, but Melchisedec priesthood is from everlasting to everlasting, the priesthood of Melchisedec had no predecessor nor successor. The Aaronic priesthood was local, temporary, and rational. However, the priesthood of Melchisedec was prior to the Levitical temporary law, and so worldwide and everlasting. The Aaronic priesthood claimed no authority over other nations, Melchisedec was a priest not only to his own city Salem but is recognized as such by Abraham, the representative of God's church and people, and the King of Sodom tacitly acquiesces in this claim to a universal priesthood. This is the significance of the title, priest of "the possessor of heaven and earth." Melchisedec is the first and the last who by God's appointment and in God's name, exercised the priesthood for Shermite and Harmite alike, the forerunner of gospel catholicity which joins under Christ all of every race.

"There is neither Jew nor Greek, there is neither bond nor free, there is neither male nor female, For ye are all on in Christ Jesus" (Gal. 3:28).

"Where there is neither Greek nor Jew, circumcision nor uncircumcision, Barbarian, Scythians, bond nor free, but Christ is all, and in all" (Col. 3:11). Melchisedec was superior to Abraham in that he blessed and received tithes from him (the giver's acknowledgment that all his property and possessions are God's) and so was superior to Levi and Aaronic priesthood which were in Abraham's loins, so the Messiah is infinitely above the Aaronic priests.

NICODEMUS

He was a member of the Sanhedrin, a council of men who ruled on Jewish law and governance. He became a friend, follower, and intellectual foil for Jesus, whose equalitarian teachings often ran counter to the Sanhedrin's rigid decrees. He was also a Pharisee, a leader within the Jewish community who toadied up to the Roman government at the time of Christ's arrest and subsequent crucifixion. He is mentioned three times in the New Testament, all in the Gospel of John. He subtly defends Jesus as the Pharisees discuss his impending arrest. Later, he helps prepare Jesus's body for burial, indicating he had become adherent to Christ and his teachings.

The first time he is mentioned, however, is in a dialogue with Jesus, and these conversations reveal some of the most aspects of Christian theology, such as the notion of being born again and the most famous reference to the divinity of Christ,

"For God so loved the world that he gave his only begotten son, that whosoever believes in Him, should not perish but have everlasting life" (John 3:16).

This detailed conversation explores the division between the old covenant's dogmatic and exclusive Jewish law and the New Covenant's spiritually inclusive concepts. But for a vital contributor to such an important passage of the New Testament, Nicodemus remains a mysterious figure. Nobody knows his hometown and relatives and where he is coming from. Some scholars have suggested he may be Nicodemus ben Carion, a Talmudic figure of wealth and martyred, and he is venerated as a saint. His name has come to be synonymous with seekers of the truth and is used as a character in many works of biblical inspiration.

JABEZ

He is only mentioned in a few verses of scripture and is known for his famous Prayer of Jabez.

"Jabez called upon the God of Israel, saying, oh you that you would bless me and enlarge my border, and that your hand might be with me and that you would keep me from harm so that it might not bring me pain? And God granted what he asked" (1Chron. 4:10).

It is a simple prayer, prayed in faith and serves as a powerful example of answered prayer and receiving blessings from the Lord. Nobody knows the mother of Jabez who named him Jabez, and nobody knows anything else about him, but a whole city was named after him, who were full of scholars and scribes.

"And the families of scribes which dwelt at Jabez, the Tiranthites, the slimeathites, and suchathites. These are the Kemites that came of Hemath, the father of the house of Rechab" (1 Chron. 2:55).

MORDECAI

The story of Mordecai takes place throughout the book of Esther. Mordecai is the cousin and guardian of Esther, a foreigner who becomes queen of Persia. Mordecai uses his position in the king's court to stand up for the oppressed people of God and foil a plot to assassinate the king.

This story plays a pivotal role in the gospel because if the Jewish people had been destroyed (like Haman desires), the story of God's saving work through the Jewish people (and eventually Christ) would have come to an end. This is what God can do through people who are obedient to Him.

THEY ARE PEOPLE OF HOLINESS

One day after a long conference in our church, I received a call from a pastor friend who told me he was watching the conference via live streaming, so I responded, "That is great." He started to laugh and asked, "What is it about this holiness you guys have been teaching, you guys really want to go to heaven?" I was speechless and astonished at his remarks, but that was a reality of things happening in the body of Christ, lack of fear of God and lack of walking in the integrity of the word.

Lack of purity in the church today, nobody wants to hear the message of holiness because we are so much in the world that the carnality of the flesh has taken over. The church has gone worldly, and the worldly has gone churchly. Thus, it is hard to distinguish between the church and the world. The church has become an entertainment center where people come and have pleasure. No wonder the church that is supposed to be a place of deliverance, transformation, and healing, has become a cemetery of dead people.

When people come to church sick, they want to go back healed. However, to our dismay, the sick comes in sick and ends up leaving even sicker. Where there is a lack of holiness, there is a dismissal of spiritual power. If there is anything we need as a church, the body of Christ, it is the fear of God. If you fear God, you abstain from anything that is not of Him. Today the body of Christ is so much into the world than they are into Christ. Sin cripples our spiritual power; sin robs us of the presence of God.

"For you are a holy people to the lord your God, the lord your God has chosen you to be a people for Himself, a special treasure above all the peoples on the face of the earth" (Deut. 7:6),

The undercover generation has been set apart for a divine purpose, to fulfill God's end-time agenda. All holiness originates with God, and believers are called to live a holy life, a life like God wants us to live.

"Therefore you shall consecrate him, for he offers the bread of your God. He shall be holy to you for I the lord, who satisfy you, am holy" (Lev. 21:8).

We serve a holy God and we must be holy people, "a cat doesn't give birth to a dog." Just as in atomic energy, modern scientists have touched a new dimension of power, so the church has to rediscover the unlimited power of the Holy Spirit. To somite the iniquity of this sin-soaked age and shatter the complacency of slumbering saints, something is really needed. Vital prayer and victorious living must come out sustained, watched in the prayer chamber. Someone says, "We must pray if we want to live a holy life!" Yes, but conversely, we must live a holy life if we want to walk in unusual power. According to David, *"Who shall ascend into the will of the Lord? He who hath clean hands and a pure heart"* (Ps. 24:3–4).

There are certain dimensions in God one cannot attain unless he has a pure heart and clean hands, and there are realms and levels of the supernatural that intellectualism, credentials, ecclesiastical honors cannot take you, not even your tithes, except holiness and righteousness.

"So that He may establish your hearts blameless in holiness before our God and Father at the coming of our Lord Jesus Christ with all his saints" (1 Thess. 3:13).

"Finally then, brethren, we urge and exhort in the Lord Jesus that you should abound more and more, just as you received from us how you ought to walk and to please God" (1 Thess. 4:1).

"But you are a chosen generation, a royal priesthood, a holy nation. His own special people, that you may proclaim the praises of Him who called you out of darkness into His marvelous light" (1 Pet. 2:9).

With numerous moral problems surrounding the present-day Pentecostal charismatic movement, I would like to affirm to you that can be full of God's fire in your bones and walk in holiness and integrity also. The consensus in the Christian community has been that charismatics and Pentecostals are shallow and morally unstable. I firmly reject this notion and would like to say that receiving the baptism of the Holy Spirit does not exclude you from a purposeful walk of integrity, which should be the quest of every believer—Pentecostal, charismatic, Baptist, or Presbyterian. Lack of holiness and integrity is not a denominational problem; it is a problem of personal sin. That is why the undercover generation is a generation that has been purified and purged with the word.

"The Adulteress will hunt for the precious life" (Prov. 6:26).

In military terms, the most dangerous enemy is the one most sought after. The undercover generation is one such enemy to darkness. It has brought a new dedication to God, a renewed interest in prayer and fasting, and a greater desire to study scripture more than ever before. It is a raging fire that sends us out beyond our religious borders. The enemy and the host of hell have not been under as much pressure as it now is under the undercover generation. This is a generation that never in the history of the church. We are, even now, witnessing and seen so many conversions to Christ since the death of its founding fathers. It is a dawning of a new day. History is being made in our generation and we know it not.

If we walk with God in the sincerity of heart, we will carry the power and the authority of God, not only that God will use us for the unimaginable. Beloved, you are part of this undercover generation, leave the world, lust, flesh, and all the carnalities and walk with him. Jesus one day appeared to me and said to me, "Son, I love you so much, and I want to use you mightily, walk with me as I walk with you. My fellow undercover generation, He wants to walk with us, but we must first walk with Him.

"For I am the Lord your God, ye shall therefore sanctify yourselves, and ye shall be holy; for I am holy, neither shall ye defile yourselves with any manner of creeping thing that creepeth upon the earth" (Lev. 11:44).

"Having therefore there promise, dearly beloved, let us cleanse ourselves from all filthiness of the flesh and spirit, perfecting holiness in the Fear of God" (2 Cor. 7:1).

We have so many promises from God. We cannot afford to lose them because of our lack of purity and holiness and not complying with his word. This is the last generation before the coming of our Lord Jesus Christ. Undercover generation, rise up and ride on the wings of integrity and holiness.

Chapter 2

The Militant Generation

This is a generation that has a military mindset, very disciplined, and regimented in every aspect of life, why because they know they are the number one target of the enemy. With respect to the enemy camp, I ask you, who would you say is the devil's greatest enemy? The generation influencing nations for Jesus Christ in a manner that has not been seen before, of course, she is the one that gets the greatest attacks. We are at war; we have an enemy. He is not concerned with private or retired army officers. He is looking for generals to strike down.

"Smite the shepherd, and the sheep shall be scattered" (Zech. 13:7).

This is a generation that comes face-to-face with the enemy's *bullet* because they step into territory or territories that are considered dangerous, why? It's because it is the enemy territory. They inflict damages on the enemy's strongholds. This is a generation purposed and determined to cover the whole world with the uncompromising preaching of God's word. This generation is targeted by the enemy for assault. The anointing God has placed upon this militant generation to help us discharge our God-given responsibility is potent, but it is also fragile. As we become visible, the devil fixes his gaze on our conduct and lifestyle. When God created man, His ultimate purpose was for man to multiply and have dominion over all of God's creation.

"And God blessed them and God said unto them, be fruitful and multiply, and replenish the earth and subdue it, and have dominion over the fish of the sea, and over the fowl of the air, and over every living thing that moveth upon the earth" (Gen. 1:28).

Dominion was and still is God's ultimate purpose for each of us. Regardless of color, race, or geographical location, we are born to have dominion, to rule over the affairs of our individual lives, and to take control and be in charge. You cannot have dominion if you are not spiritually militant and aggressive and bombarding the camp of the enemy, persistently through warfare. This is a generation that battles the enemy and stops the vomits of hell on its knees. They pray through until their breakthrough. When you are consumed by His will and purpose, it steals your appetite for food and drives you to the altar to conceive the objects of your prayer, then comes the victory, the breakthrough. When I was in high school, we learned about reflection and light. I will never forget the experiment my science teacher conducted years ago. He used a magnifying glass to arrest the rays of the sun and filtered them through the glass.

As long as the light rays were all over the paper, there was no specific effect, but when the beam was concentrated into one sharp ray, the paper would burn. His experiment has remained fresh in my mind. I learned that when you concentrate on one thing, you will penetrate every obstacle, and your work shall become visible. Our inability to be militant in our prayer on our part has hindered God from honoring our *universal prayers* without warfare. Our prayers are ceremonial. Without militancy, our prayers lack tenacity. Without regiment, spiritually, one can never overcome opposition. Lack of vibrancy in our warfare which is the militant spirit we cannot prevail, but thank God for the undercover generation is a militant generation. We are called to dominate and not to be dominated.

From the beginning, the original intent of God is for man to have and walk in dominion, which was the divine agenda. Each of us is engaged in the spiritual battle between God's forces on the universe and the forces of darkness, the devil. The spirit of the Lord is moving to and fro throughout the whole earth, selecting a certain type of persons to serve in God's army, one whose heart is perfect toward God. Whenever the Holy Spirit finds such character in a soldier, he delights to show Himself strong on that person's behalf, openly manifesting His power and approval in that person's life and ministry.

But let there be no mistake. Even though the rewards are many, the prospect of fighting spiritual battles is never easy. The desire to serve Him with a perfect heart takes all a person has to give. The Bible tells us that Abraham was that kind of soldier and Job. Scripture says that they had just such a heart. They accepted the challenges facing them and reached the climax of spiritual growth. But wait! You say first things first, I am not Abraham or Job, and how can I possibly have a heart that is perfect toward God? If that is what it takes to prepare for my role in spiritual ballet, if the rules of engagement can be embraced only by one whose heart is perfect toward God, I might face defeat before I start!

Don't forget you cannot be militant if you are walking in disobedience to the word. No, you are not Abraham, but you can accept a fresh challenge from God. And you are not Job, but you can have a right attitude toward God and a right attitude toward evil. You see, we will discover that there is no neutrality in perfection toward God. A soldier in His army does not compromise with anything that is displeasing to Him, you must be absolutely committed to obedience, no matter what it costs. And be reminded, as every soldier knows, it does cost something to be approved by God! We are all coming to the point of the consummation of the purpose of God for the ages.

And the message of God for every person who is gone to take his place in what God is doing is this "walk before Me and be perfect."

This is how we will fulfill our roles in the spiritual battle, day-to-day trials now and greater battles to come. Close to two decades now, I have tried to help people with innumerable problems in their lives. Eventually, I have come to a surprising conclusion our basic problem as human beings is that we do not realize how valuable we are. As we have been enlisted in this militant generation, we need to focus more on the way God sees us that the way we see ourselves. We often miss the call to join in the great battle because we think that we cannot make the grade.

Consequently, we make the most tragic mistakes. We are like a person who is legally an heir to a vast fortune, but we sell off our entire inheritance for something incomparably less valuable—a right of sense, a venture into the world of drugs, a drunken party, a crooked financial scheme. Or we may value ourselves a little higher, perhaps seeking some prestigious position in politics or the entertainment world or even some high ecclesiastical office. Yet for all its prestige, it does not compare with the value of our inheritance which we give in exchange for it.

God wants to move in power in our lives. He wants us to move victoriously through the years ahead, learning more about Him and learning more about ourselves. Thus we will cover a lot of ground as we take our places in the spiritual battle raging around us. We will learn how a soldier's character is developed and what to do when facing tests. We will enter the training camp of the greatest teacher and helper on earth, the Holy Spirit. Then we will move into battle in the *heavenlies*, learning many schemes of the enemy. And finally we will take up our stations and put to the test the character that endures. Our goal is to prepare. Let us start now, we have prevailed.

Chapter 3

Mighty Warriors

The spirit of God is sounding an alarm throughout the nations of the earth today. By His spirit, he is calling together His end-time spiritual warriors to pick up their mighty weapon of prayer to travail, to weep, to intercede. We are living in the time known as the *climax of the ages* when God is going to unify all things in heaven and earth and bring them together and consummate them in Christ.

"Having made known unto us the mystery of His will according to His good pleasure which he hath purposed in himself: That in the dispensation of the fullness of time he might gather together in one all things in Christ both which are in heaven, and which are on earth, even in him" (Eph. 1:9–10).

As God's warriors for the end-time, we must be spiritually alert, and God is also calling us to act!

As we prepare for the end-time harvest, we must take our position as end-time spiritual warriors, God does not want us to sit back with our hands folded. He does not want us to become so caught up with the cares and worries of this life, which we fail to see the signs of the end-time harvest, which we fail to prepare, that we fail to warn those around us before it's too late.

The spirit of God is sounding an alarm throughout the earth, gathering together mighty and time spiritual warriors who will *"blow the trumpet in Zion and sound an alarm."* In our churches today we rejoice, clap our hands, and dance as we sing, *"Blow the trumpet in Zion, Zion sound the alarm on my holy mountain, blow the trumpet in Zion, Zion sound the alarm."* But sounding of the trumpet is not a call to rejoicing, it is calling together a *solemn* assembly. As we see the day of the Lord drawing near, we must sound the alarm and pick up our weapon of prayer and begin to intercede. God instructed Moses to make two silver trumpets, which were to be blown by Aaron and the priests to call together an assembly of the people (Num. 10:1–10). Today, God is calling His end-time *warriors*, you and me, to *"blow the trumpet in Zion, sanctify a fast, call a solemn assembly"* (Joel 2:15).

As end-time mighty and spiritual warriors, it is up to us to pick up our mighty weapon of prayer and intercede; it is up to us to lead the way! After we have entered into this time of fasting and prayer in repentance, we must then pick up our weapon of prayer and begin to intercede with the lost in our families, in our communities, and in our nations. As the day of the Lord draws near, our position as end-time spiritual warriors is standing in the gap, interceding for the lost. As mighty warriors, we are intercessors. We must stand in the gap and pray petitions or pleads on behalf of another. If we are intercessors, we are supposed to intervene between two parties. As intercessors, we must penetrate deep into the realm of the spirit in times of prayer and fasting on behalf of the sin that surrounds us.

We must cry out and plead with God on behalf of those who are bound by Satan. This type of intercession, I am referring to is not the *normal* five-minute prayer, where we give God a list of names of people we would like to see saved and delivered out of Satan's hand, the type of intercession God is calling us to do is much more than that. It involves getting on our faces before God in prayer—mourning and weeping and travailing, waiting before Him, and not letting go until the work has been done. It requires us to be willing to stand in the gap on behalf of others as well as entire nations.

JESUS INTERCEDED, TRAVAILED, AND MOURNED BEFORE THE BATTLE WAS WON.

Jesus's entire life was an act of intercession; he stood in the gap between God and man. Isaiah prophesied concerning Him, *"Now the Lord saw, And it was displeasing in His sight that there was no justice. And He saw that, there was no man, and was astonished that there was no one to intercede; Then his own brought salvation to Him; and his righteousness*

upheld him. And He put on righteousness like a breast plate, And a helmet

of salvation on His head; And He puts on garments of vengeance for clothing,

And wrapped Himself with zeal as a mantle" (Isa. 59:15–17, NAS).

Jesus, seeing there was no intercessor, no one to stand in the gap for

the sins of the world, put on His spiritual armor and came to earth to

bring salvation. As our intercessor, Jesus identified with man. He did

not elevate Himself, above us, but humbled Himself and was made in

the likeness of men (Phil. 2:7). In identifying with us, he was willing

to lay down His divine attributes and become like us, sharing the same

human nature and being made like us in all respects.

> *For as much then as the children are partakers of flesh and*
> *blood, he also himself likewise took part of the same, that*
> *through death he might destroy him that had the power of*
> *death, that is, the devil, For verily he took not on him in*
> *nature of angels; but he took on him the seed of Abraham.*
> *Wherefore in all things it behooved him to be made*
> *like unto his brethren, that he might be a merciful and*
> *faithful high priest in things pertaining to God, to make*
> *reconciliation for the sins of the people.* (Heb. 2:14,16–17)

As our intercessors, He was willing to stand in our stead. As sinners,

we were alienated, separated from God. Man had turned his back on

God and chose to follow his own ways to follow after his own man-made gods. We were worthy of death. But Jesus, our intercessor, was willing to come to earth and stand in the gap. He was willing to give His own life to die in our place, that we might be reconciled to God.

Throughout His ministry on earth, He was ever interceding for man, bringing them to the father forgiving men's sins, restoring both body and spirit. As our intercessor, He wept over these and judgment that was coming because the people would not heed His warning. On His triumphal entry into Jerusalem, where He was going to offer Himself as a sacrifice for the sins of the world, Jesus wept. Can you see Jesus there amid the cries of "Hosanna; blessed is he that cometh in the name of the Lord" as He stops on the hillside overlooking Jerusalem? As He looks upon the city, tears begin to pour from His eyes. He begins to sob and cry as if His heart is broken. As He weeps, He cries for Jerusalem, *"If you, even you, had only known on this day what would bring you peace, but now it is hidden from your eyes, The days will come upon when your enemies will build an embankment against you and encircle you and hem you in on every side. They will dash you to the ground you and the children within your walls. They will not leave one stone on another, because you did not recognize the time of God's coming to you"* (Luke 19:42-44, NIV).

Later, after proclaiming the judgments that were coming upon Jerusalem, He cried out in anguish, *"O Jerusalem, Jerusalem, you who kill the prophets and stone those sent to you, how often have I longed to gather your children together, as a hen gathers her chicks under her wings, but you were not willing. Look, your house is left to you obsolete. For I tell you, you will not see me again until you say, Blessed is he who comes in the name of the Lord"* (Matt. 23:37–39, NIV).

As our intercessor, Jesus travailed on our behalf. Our salvation was not easily acquired. It cost Jesus everything, and it was not easy. In the garden of Gethsemane, Jesus wrestled, struggled, and travailed in prayer. Isaiah prophesied concerning His travailing.

"Yet it pleased the Lord to bruise him, he hath him to grief; when thou shalt make his soul an offering for sin . . . He shall see of the travail of his soul, and be satisfied" (Isa. 53:10–11).

The word "travail" is taken from a Jewish word which means "to writhe in pain". It is compared with the indescribable pain a woman experiences in the last stages of labor, before giving birth to her child. As our intercessor, Jesus took our place there on the cross. As the Roman soldiers beat him mercilessly, He stood there in our place. As they nailed His hands and feet to the cross and placed the cross in the ground, Jesus was "standing in the gap" for you and me. There on the cross, He was interceding, reconciling us back to God. He took our shame, our rejection, our pain, and our sins upon Himself. God spoke through Isaiah the prophet, *"There will I divide him a portion with the great, and he shall divide the spoil with the strong, because he hath poured out his soul unto death, and he was numbered with the transgressors; and he bore the sin of many, and made intercession for the transgressors"* (Isa. 53:12).

As our intercessor, Jesus ascended into heaven and is now seated at the right hand of the Father where He is standing in the gap, making intercession for us. He is aware of our pain and suffering. He sees all our sins. And He is there in heaven, interceding to the Father on our behalf.

"But this man (Jesus), because he continueth ever, hath an unchangeable priesthood. Wherefore he is able to save them to the outermost that come unto God by him, seeing he ever liveth to make intercession for them" (Heb. 7:24–25).

Chapter 4

Divine Qualification to the Army of Warriors

One thing we must know and understand is that God doesn't select and recruit as men does. Men look at the outward appearance and countenance, but the Lord took unto the heart and the spirit.

"For my thoughts are not your thoughts neither are your ways, declares the Lord. As heavens are higher than the earth, so are my ways higher than your ways and my thoughts than your thoughts" (Isa. 55:8–9, NIV).

"But the Lord said unto Samuel, Look not on his countenance, or on the height of his stature, because I have refused him; For the Lord seeth not as man seeth; For man looketh on the outward appearance, but the Lord looketh on the heart" (1 Sam. 16:7).

God doesn't judge as men do; that is why those who define you must redefine you because what they think. That wasn't what God thought of you; to them, you are out and disqualified, but God said, "My son, my daughter you are in." As I was pondering on how God recruits and qualifies, it reminded me of the account of Gideon and his army in *Judges 6–8*.

At this time, Israel had fallen into sin and idolatry, and as a judgment, God permitted vast hordes of Midianites to invade her land each year and rob her of her harvest. One day while Gideon was furtively threshing wheat in a winepress to hide it from the Midianites, the *"angel of the Lord"* appeared to him and said *"The Lord is with you, you mighty man of valor!"* (Judg. 6:11–12). As we learned in the last chapter, this angel who appeared to man was often the preincarnate of Christ. Obviously the Lord saw Gideon quite differently from the way that he saw himself. Gideon saw himself as young, weak, and ineffective. The Lord hailed him as a "mighty man of valor."

As I mentioned earlier, we need to be less concerned with how we see ourselves and be more concerned with how God sees us. In Christ, each one of us is a *"new man . . . Created according to God in true righteousness and holiness"* (Eph. 4:24).

Viewing ourselves like this will inevitably affect the way we engage in warfare. The Lord commissioned Gideon to lead Israel in the battle against Midianites. In response, Gideon assembled an army by the well of Harod with the Midianites encamped to the north. What were the numbers on both sides?

Gideon's army: 32,000

Midianite army: 135,000

"Thus Gideon with 32,000 men" (see Judg. 7:3) *"faces 135,000 Midianites"* (see Judg. 8:10). He was outnumbered more than four to one. So imagine Gideon's reaction when the Lord told him, *"The people who are with you are too many"* (Judg. 7:2).

The Lord instructed Gideon to send away all those in his army who were fearful and afraid. As a result, 22,000 men departed, and Gideon was left with 10,000. At this point, he was outnumbered more than thirteen to one. But God was not finished! To Gideon's astonishment, He said, *"The people are still too many"* (verse 4). Then He instructed Gideon to bring his men down to the water so that he might test there by the way they drank from the water. Those who went down on both knees to drink were eliminated. Those who lapped like a dog passed the test (see Judg. 7:4–7).

4.1 One Essential Character Requirement of This Army

The test focused on one single character requirement, VIGILANCE! Picture first those who drank in the normal way. Laying aside their shield from the left arm and the spear or sword from the right arm, they went down on both knees and buried their faces in the water. In this posture, they were totally vulnerable to a surprise attack. They could not see any approaching enemy, neither did they have their weapons ready to use. In the time it took to get themselves ready, the enemy would have overcome them. What about those who lapped like dogs?

When a dog drinks, it does not bury its nose in the water. It stretches out its tongue and laps the water up into its mouth, usually splashing some water around. How then should we picture the men who lapped? Judges 7:6 says that with a cupped hand, they scooped up the water to their mouths. In other words, they went down on one knee only. Retaining their shield on their left arm, with the right arm they set down their spear or sword beside them. In this posture, they remained alert, watching constantly for any surprise attacks. Their shields were already in position, and they could instantly pick up their spear or sword and have it ready to use.

There was no possibility of the enemy catching them off guard. Only three hundred of Gideon's men passed the second test. They were outnumbered 450 to 1! I can picture some of those who were dismissed saying to themselves, *"Well thank God we're out of that! Gideon must be crazy.*

"What difference does it make how a man drinks water? Let's see what will become of him and the idiots who stay with him". In the outcome, of course, Gideon and his three hundred engineered a surprise attack that threw the Midianites into confusion. After that, other Israelites rallied behind Gideon and inflicted total defeat on the Midianites.

The proportions are illuminating. Only three hundred men fulfilled the qualifications for the initial attack. But once they broke through, thousands of Israelites were eager to pursue the fleeing Midianites. This whole account illustrates how different God's ways are from ours. Left to himself, Gideon would surely have concluded, "The people with me are too few, I need to get reinforcements." In the end, Gideon was left with fewer than one out of a hundred of those who originally joined him. For God, the question is not "how many people?" but "what kind of people?"

In the light of this account, we each need to make a personal assessment. In the army God is gathering today, would I be one of the few who qualify? Or would I be like the 22,000 who were eliminated because they gave way to fear or like the 9,700 who laid down their weapons and buried their faces in the water to drink? It is easy and often normal to bury our faces in the business of daily living; to be absorbed in all the practical needs that confront us every day, to forget that we are in a spiritual conflict with unseen forces of darkness who are continually watching for an opportunity to catch us unprepared.

To maintain unceasing vigilance in every situation demands conscious, personal discipline. It gets beyond all our normal concepts of Christian conduct and morality. Yet the New Testament clearly warns us, *"Be sober, be vigilant; because your adversary the devils walks about like a roaring Lion, seeking whom he may devour"* (1 Pet. 5:8).

If we ignore this warning, we become vulnerable to subtle, unpredictable assaults of Satan. This could apply to many different areas: family, relationships, business activities, vacations, special celebrations, educational opportunities. We can participate in all of these, but we must not bury our faces in any of them. Remember in Gideon's army, only one out of a hundred qualified! Would the proportions be different today? Once we pass the test of vigilance, that is just the beginning. We look now at the next steps in building the character of a soldier.

4.2 The Weapon of Purity Is a Requirement for This Army

"Now may the God of peace Himself sanctify you completely; and may your whole spirit, soul, and body be preserved blameless at the coming of tour Lord, Jesus Christ" (1Thess 5:23).

It is Paul's prayer that Christians are completely sanctified, and he then specifies the three areas that make up total human personality: spirit, soul, and body. The distinctions of each of these three elements of our personalities are little understood by most Christians. Yet the Bible, as a unique kind of mirror, reveals their nature and interrelationship and shows us how each is intended to function. Failure to follow all that we see in this mirror exposes us to much inner frustration and disharmony.

In the initial creation of man, God said, *"Let us create man in our image"* *and according to our likeness"* (Gen. 1:26). Image refers to our outward appearance. In a way that is not true of any other creature, humans reflect the outward appearance of God. It was appropriate, therefore, that when the son of God came to dwell on the earth, it was in the form of a human, not an ox or a beetle, and not even in the form of some heavenly creature, such as a seraph. Likeness refers to our inner nature. Scripture refers to God as a triune being: Father, Son, and Spirit. Likewise, it reveals that man is a triune being, consisting of spirit, soul, and body.

The accounts of man's creation reveal how his triune nature came into being, *"And the Lord God formed man of the dust of the ground and breathed into his nostrils the breath of life; and man became a living being"* more correctly, a living soul (Gen. 2:7). Man's spirit came from the inbreathing of God. His body was formed from clay, transformed into living human flesh. Instantly he became a living soul. The soul that formed is the ego, the individual personality. It is unusually defined as consisting of three elements: the will, the intellect, and the emotions. It has the responsibility for making personal decisions and expresses itself in three phrases, *"I want," "I think," and "I feel."* Unless touched by the supernatural grace of God, all of human behavior is controlled by these three motivations.

The Divine Manual for the End-Time Army

In an earthly army, a soldier who is enlisted is provided with appropriate weapons and then receives training to make him or her proficient in their use. It is imperative for us as soldiers in the Lord's end-time army that we, too, become proficient in the use of the weapons that God has provided: the blood of the lamb and the word of our testimony. We must learn how to testify appropriately concerning each provision made for us through the blood of Jesus. I outline below a training manual on how to appropriate the various provisions made for us through the blood of Jesus.

If you will familiarize yourself with the passages of scripture or better still, commit them to memory. You will be prepared to take part in the vast spiritual conflict with which the present age will close.

The blood of Jesus cries out continually to God in heaven on my behalf (see Heb. 12:24).

Through the blood of Jesus, I have boldness to enter into the presence of God (see Heb. 10:19).

Through the blood of Jesus, I am justified, made righteous, "just as if I'd never sinned" (see Rom. 5:9).

Through the blood of Jesus, I am satisfied, made holy, set apart to God (see Heb. 13:12).

Through the blood of Jesus, I am continually being cleansed from all sin (see 1 John 1:7).

Through the blood of Jesus, all my sins are forgiven (see 1 John 1:9).

Through the blood of Jesus, I am redeemed out of the hand of the devil (see Eph. 1:7).

We overcome Satan when we testify personally to what the word of God says the blood of Jesus does for us (see Rev. 12:11).

One Most Important Requirement

Revelation 12:11 closes with one distinguishing characteristic of all those who emerge victorious from this conflict: *"They did not love their lives to the death."* How shall we apply this to ourselves? It means that for us it is more important to do the will of God than to stay alive.

If we should ever find ourselves in a situation where obeying God will cost us our lives, then we will obey God. Probably all of us will actually have to make a clear-cut choice. But the decisive issue is our commitment. This imparts a quality to our testimony that makes it a weapon against which Satan has no defense. We each need, therefore, to confront ourselves with this question. Can I truthfully say to myself that I do not live my life to death? Now that we have studied many schemes of the enemy, let us take up our station in this battle and put to test the character that endures.

Chapter 5

The Indefatigable Army

We have moved out unto the battlefield of the heart and mind to expose and defeat Satan and his army of deluding, seducing, lying spirits who are attacking God's people today in a massive counterattack to stop the advance of the church into his territory! We are not hiding in fear or *"holding the fort."* We are not running from Satan in fear. We are pursuing him and seizing the victory that belongs to us!

By His spirit, God is thrusting us out in new strength to confront Satan, demolish his strongholds, and press the battle against him until he has to retreat. God is teaching us how to wage war. Notice what the great warrior King David said as he praised God for giving him victory over all his enemies, *"God is my strength and power, and he maketh my way perfect. He maketh my feet like hinds feet, and setteth me upon my high places. He teacheth my hands to war so that a bow of steel is broken by mine arms. Thou hast also given me the shield of thy salvation; and they gentleness hath made me great. Thou has enlarged my steps under me; so that my feet did not slip. I have pursued mine enemies, and destroyed them; and turned not again until I had consumed them. And I have consumed them, and wounded them, that they could not arise, yea, they are fallen under my feet"* (2 Sam. 22:33–39).

David knew the secret to victory. He pursued his enemies and did not turn to the left or right or stop waging war until he had consumed them. We are going out to fight against Satan and his principalities with this same determination and spiritual aggressiveness. God is pouring new strength into us. He has taught our hands to war and has strengthened and equipped us to pursue our enemies until they subdued and crushed under our feet. There is an army of believers being gathered and equipped these days, who will be skilled in all the weapons of spiritual warfare. They will be those who have an understanding of the times and insight into the ways of God concerning kingdom conquest.

Their discernment is the spiritual things and submission to the leading of the spirit will them great advantage over previous generations of warriors both in the kingdom of light and the kingdom of darkness. They view the kingdom of God not as a term or an idea to be debated, but as the powerful reign of Jesus, the king of kings and lord of lords. To become enlisted in this end-time army, one must go through the boot camp of the Holy Spirit and waive all the carnal ways of warfare burned out of him. No allegiance to the flesh can be tolerated, or defeat in the heat of battle will be inevitable. God has given the spirits the power to burn all the fleshy desires out of these front liners and baptize them totally in his fire.

"I indeed baptize you with water unto repentance: but he that cometh after me is mightier than I, whole shoes I am not worthy to bear: he shall baptize you with the Holy Ghost, and with fire: Whose pan is in his hand, and he will thoroughly purge his floor, and gather is wheat into the garner; but he will burn up the chaff with unquenchable fire" (Matt. 3:11–12).

Shadrach, Meshach, and Abednego were thrown into the fiery furnace, yet the only that burned was the cord that held them bound. God's fire set people free. When we are free of self, free of the lusts and carnal desires that weigh us down, then the life of God can freely flow through us. When the baptism of fire burns through us, it will eliminate all the soulish and selfish clutter so that we can be victorious over the fiery darts that come against us.

"For as much then as Christ hath suffered for us in the flesh, arm yourselves likewise with the same mind: For he, that hat suffered in the flesh hath ceased from sin" (1 Pet. 4:1).

As we allow the spirit of God to burn all the fleshly chaff out of our lives, it will result in a deathlike process. A funeral for the flesh will take place. Then God will have us right where He wants us. Now He can enlist us into His army of overcomers, and we will be armed to defeat the enemy on every score.

How does one sign up for enlistment into this team of special forces in the kingdom? The simple key to finding God is to seek Him. He is not interested in the performance of outward shows. When an individual develops a disciplined lifestyle of setting himself apart from the world to seek the Lord, the fire of God will be present, both to destroy and to build. The Lord told Joshua to tell the people of God. "Sanctify yourselves for tomorrow, I shall do signs and wonders among you". The word sanctify means to "set apart".

"A good soldier does not entangle himself with the affairs of this world" (2 Tim. 2:4).

"He is one who must sometimes endure hardship" (v3).

A good soldier is under authority and seeks to please the one who made him a soldier. It can be so easy to give in the will of the flesh or go the way of the world. When we turn to God with all our heart, making a determined effort to seek Him and His wisdom, He will keep us in the hour of testing. Soldiers who have first committed themselves to peaceful moments of communication with their captains who can fully wield their swords. The commander in chief will give the instruction, reproof, encouragement, and revelation necessary to produce boldness for the battle. Suffering in the flesh means disciplining ourselves to write the Lord's orders on the tablets of our hearts and minds. This need not be a burdensome process for in seeking the Lord, we will find grace sufficient for every need. The army of God is led into battle with peace of heart, knowing the battle has been secured through Jesus's death and resurrection. The strategy for daily victory awaits those who seek His face.

Chapter 6

Army of Fearless Warriors

"And of the Gadites there separated themselves unto David into the hold to the wilderness men of mighty and men of war fit for the battles, that could handle shield and buckler, whose faces were like the faces of lions, and were as swift as the roes upon the mountain" (1 Chron. 12:8).

The army of fearless warriors are like the Gadites men; they are wilderness men of might.

Remember that it is only the "wilderness men: that entered the promised land." When God delivered the children of Israel from Egypt into the promised land, the original generation that was delivered by the mighty hand of Jehovah did not make it to the promised land. It was those who were born in the wilderness that made it to the promised land.

These wilderness men are also men of war, fit for battle. If our earthly army recruits men who are physically it and without any deformity, how much more our heavenly father who is the God of war. He will recruit able bodies, spiritual and physical men who are spiritually infused and injected with divine boldness and capabilities to apprehend the strategies of the devil. These men can also handle a shield and a buckler. Their faces are like the face of lions and they are as swift as the roses upon the mountains.

According to the scriptures, Jesus Christ is the lion of the tribe of Judah. This means that these men have the likeness of Christ and are in conformity with His image. These are the people who have been overshadowed by the image and glory of Christ. You can never be part of this army if you do not have the resemblance of Christ. You can never be a good soldier if you do not know how to handle a gun. These warriors are competent men, capable of handling scriptures and more able to appropriate the blood and the name of Jesus Christ in spiritual warfare.

"Benaiah the son of Jehoiafa, the son of a valiant man of Kabzeel, who had done many acts; he slew two lion like men of Moab: also he went down and slew a lion in a pit in a snowy day" (1 Chron. 11:22).

One very important thing about these warriors and fighters is that they know that it is "not by their might or power, but it is by the spirit of the Lord." They, therefore, go to battle in the name of the Lord knowing not to trust in the arm of the flesh. They also know that *"the name of the lord is a strong tower, the righteous run into it and are safe."*

David, the man after God's heart, knows a secret which Saul and his three older brothers—Eliab, Abinadab, and Shammah—did not know the secret of trusting and having faith in the name of the Lord. With this knowledge, David was able to say to Goliath face-to-face, *"Thou comest to me with a sword and with a spear, and with a shield: but I come to thee in the name of the Lord of hosts, the God of the armies of Israel, whom thou has defied . . . And all this assemble shall know that the LORD saveth not with sword and spear: For the battle is the Lord's and he will give you into our hands"* (1 Sam. 17:45, 47).

The Bible also records in 1 Chronicles 12:33, *"Of Zebulun, such as wet forth to battle, expert in war with all instruments of war, fifty thousand which could keep rank. They were not o double heart."*

These were specialized warriors who were experts and strategists of war. They only take instructions from their commander in chief, Jesus Christ. This explains why *"they were not of double heart."*

The army of God that is rising up today is a mighty army of people with the spirit of Joshua and Caleb. They are bold, faithful, and wholly dedicated to the Lord. This army had four important characteristics. First, they have godly aggressiveness. These warriors know they were created for spiritual warfare and they enjoy it. When the trumpet sounds for war, they run to the battle rather than complain about how hard it is! Because they know their place in the kingdom realm, they have confidence in the greater one who overcomes the world through their faith. They also have boldness before the throne of grace, and they know how to bring things down from heaven onto the earth.

Secondly, they have godly attitudes. Remember, your attitude will determine our altitude.

Kingdom warriors never say, "It's impossible, I can't, or I won't" to the Word of God. They believe they can do all things through Christ who strengthens them. One thing God's army must understand is that He only strengthens us when we are fighting His war, not ours. Many are fighting circumstances and problems that don't have anything to do with what God is doing.

Circumstances will do one of two things: they will make us better, or they will make us bitter. A godly attitude will deliver us from the "I'll do what I want" mentality.

"The wise in heart will receive commandments: but a prating (babbling) fool shall fall" (Prov. 10:8).

Godly attitudes bring maturity in relationships involving forgiveness, humility, and compassion.

Thirdly, this army has godly associations. God's end-time knows that they will become like those with whom they spend the most time. Associations will either assist or assault us. They will either build us up or pull us down. Never associate will the devil's coffers. Get involved with people who are going somewhere with God. Godly associations also mean being in covenant with a local church that knows its place in God's army and is hearing what the spirit is saying. Whenever the doors are open these warriors show up for the battle, they take their place in the move of God and are fitly framed in the body, supplying their part.

Fourthly, these believers have godly applications. True veterans in God's army put themselves in positions where they must obey God's word. A godly application of God's word is obedience. Obedience is the only way to experience the kingdom. A godly application sees the opportunity for victory, not the obstacle for defeat. It sees the potential, not the problem. The more we do what we know, the more we know what to do. God is challenging His army in this hour to implicit obedience. God is raising up an army like Gideon's. There are tests to pass, but the church will not be trampled. Rather, it will be triumphant if it continues to inquire of the Lord and obey His order.

Requirement for Warfare

"Jesus is preparing an army that 'no man could number'" (Rev. 7:9).

His soldiers are suited up in fine "linen clean and white" (Rev. 19:8). They are clothed with the holiness of God. His soldiers have allowed that purging fire to burn in them and cleanse them.

They hate sin, love righteousness, and are filled with his compassion. God doesn't want us to be a sick, tired, and worn army. He needs an army filled with zeal for His house, fired up and ready to fight.

In Deuteronomy chapter twenty, the Lord announces the requirements for warfare. He describes the four types of people who were not to enter battle lest they should die. When applied spiritually to the army of the Lord, it can make a tremendous change in a soldier who desires in the fight of faith.

> *When thou goest out to battle against thine enemies, and seest horses, and chariots, and a people more than thou, be not afraid of them: for the lord thy God is with thee, which brought thee up out of the land of Egypt. And it shall be, when ye are come right unto the battle, that the priest shall approach and speak unto the people, and shall say unto them. Hear, O Israel, ye approach this day, unto battle against your enemies. Let not your hearts Faint, fear not, and do not tremble, neither be ye terrified because of them; for the Lord your God is He that goeth with you, to fight for you against you enemies, to save you.*
>
> *And the officers shall speak unto the people, saying, what man is there that hath built a new house, and hath not dedicated it? Let him go and return to his house*

lest he die in the battle, and another man dedicate it.
(Deut. 20:1–5)

The first category of soldiers, God says will have trouble fighting will be those who have built a new house and "have not dedicated it." In the spirit, we must understand the necessity of dedicating our house (our physical temple) to the Lord. Our thoughts, desires, and the motives of our heart must be yielded to the Lord and His divine principles so the devil will not have an open door to steal, kill, or destroy God's soldiers. Soulful ideas and thoughts can captivate and entertain, but the individual who has yielded to the Lord in his heart and prayer life will find great victory in the day of warfare.

Another area of dedication is to the house of God or the local assembly. Everyone who desires protection in spiritual warfare must be joined in a covenant with (submitted to) a local church. Some of the greatest warfare we experience is enduring or putting up with other soldiers in the army of God. Great victory and maturity come when we stay long enough in a local assembly to work through the differences and establish life-long, permanent, godly relationships. The anointing flows through people, not church buildings and flashy programs.

The body must come together joint to joint in God's divine order to release the flow of life throughout it. Left alone, the believer will die in battle. One of the greatest revelations, the body can have is of the need of each member for the other others.

"And what man is he that hath planted a vineyard, and hath not yet eaten of it? Le him also go and return unto his house, lest he die in the battle, and another man eat of it" (Deut. 20:6).

The second category includes those who do not cultivate the fruit of the spirit in their lives. Every believer has a vineyard planted in his heart. When we are born again, the love of God is shed abroad in our hearts by the Holy Spirit. All the fruit of the spirit (love, joy, peace, patience, and self-control) are designed to be developed and eaten by the individual harvesting the fruit. The fruit of the spirit is not only pleasant to behold, but it is essential as a weapon of war.

"Perfect love will cast out all fear" (1 John 4:18).

"It is not jealous or judgmental, therefore we will stand united as one body. It will place us far above all principalities, powers, and rulers of darkness. Faith will allow us to overcome the world" (1 John 5:4).

Joy is the strength of our life. A man without self-control is like a city built without walls. Patience will undergird faith when the going is rough! Do we think we can win the war without these fruits actively working in our lives? God exhorted those without fruits to return home lest they die in battle. When God is finished with His army, it's going to be as gentle as a dove but as wise as a serpent.

Lightning Source UK Ltd.
Milton Keynes UK
UKHW012015070621
385112UK00007B/680/J